TEA GARDENS

PLACES TO MAKE AND TAKE TEA

TEA GARDENS

ANN LOVEJOY | *Photographs by Allan Mandell*

CHRONICLE BOOKS

SAN FRANCISCO

Library of Congress Cataloging-in-Publication Data:

Lovejoy, Ann, 1951–
    Tea gardens : places to make and take tea / by Ann Lovejoy ;
photographs by Allan Mandell
    120 p.   17.8 x 20.4 cm.
    Includes index.
    ISBN 0-8118-1905-1 (hc)
    1. Tea gardens. 2. Tea.   I. Title.
SB454.3.T43L68   1998
712'.6—dc21   97-49826
                             CIP

Printed in Hong Kong
Designed by Jean Sanchirico

Distributed in Canada by Raincoast Books
8680 Cambie Street, Vancouver, British Columbia V6P 6M9

10   9   8   7   6   5   4   3   2   1

Chronicle Books
85 Second Street
San Francisco, California 94105

Web Site: www.chroniclebooks.com

TEATIME

I LEARNED TO TAKE DELIGHT IN THE PLEASURE

AFFORDED BY A CUP OF TEA. . . . A SIMPLE CUP OF TEA

HAS OFTEN BEEN THE ONLY SPARK NEEDED TO MAKE

AN ACQUAINTANCE, INAUGURATING A BOND OF

FRIENDSHIP THAT COULD LAST A LIFETIME.

P. Bruneton | *En solitaire dans l'Himalaya*

The idea of making and taking tea in the garden is as old as tea itself. In China and Japan, the tradition of enjoying both herbal and medicinal teas in a garden setting has literally thousands of years' standing. Indeed, nearly five thousand years ago, the legendary Yellow Emperor of China (or more probably his court physician) wrote a treatise describing how to use herbal teas to treat everything from the common cold to chronic pain and even diseases now recognized as heart attack and diabetes.

The idea of taking tea for pleasure alone has equally deep roots. Asian traditions all value the contemplative qualities of good tea well taken, and Eastern cultures have long stressed the psychological importance of creating garden places in which tea may be fully savored. Perhaps these roots are as deep as human history, for recent discoveries have revealed that in ancient Chinese cave-dwelling sites, prehistoric people collected certain wild tea herbs still in common use. We cannot know whether they, too, brewed teas from them to sip at the mouth of those protective caves, perhaps admiring a fading sunset or greeting each fresh morning with a ceremonial cup. It's fun to speculate on such ideas, and they are not entirely far-fetched, for it is very certain that teas and infusions are nearly as integral a part of human culture as hot water.

In Europe, too, teas and tea gardens have a long and healthy history. In 1633, John Gerard, a famous herbalist whose master work, *The Herbal*, is still in print, included hundreds of herbal tea remedies in his enormous tome. Few, if any, were original to him and most already had the sheen of ages on them. Doctors, wise women, and old wives had tales and track records that went back into the dimness of time for herbal teas that were both curative and tasty.

The concept of taking tea out of doors, drawing spiritual and physical refreshment from contact with the natural, was intrinsic to the development of Asian tea gardens. The idea was slower to spread in the West, where man's urge to dominate nature made that basic relationship more antagonistic than healing. Not until the late 1700s did it become fashionable to picnic and take tea in the garden or countryside. Once begun, however, teahouses, gazebos, and picturesque follies quickly became all the rage, and since then the practice has never fallen completely out of favor.

These days, the idea of serving lovely teas in the garden evokes dreams of the golden '40s, when nearly all middle class homes had helpers to carry the trays and tidy up afterward. Teatime, by English tradition, is supposed to be at four or five o'clock, times when many of us are either still at work or busily car-pooling tired and hungry children between school and lessons. We are much more likely to need substantial, healthy snacks which can be eaten on the run at that hour.

Mornings are also all too often rushed, as children prepare for school and adults for a day on the job. Half the time, I discover my morning tea sitting stone cold where I left it hours earlier as I raced around trying to find misplaced homework or somebody's socks. I love the idea of morning tea, but making time for the reality of it is a significant and worthy challenge.

If tea-taking seems to belong to a more leisurely age, perhaps the concept simply needs an update to make it fit comfortably into modern life. Certainly, leisure is among the most desirable commodities of our day; our whole society acknowledges the irony that we are constantly hustling through our work so we can grab some time to relax. Real relaxation is rare in our culture; when we do find a few free minutes, we are more apt to spend it exercising or pursuing some purposeful project than indulging in unstructured, dreamy activities like tea-drinking.

Taking tea is about making time instead of grabbing it, and about genuinely relaxing instead of simply giving lip service to the idea. How we accomplish this is less important than that we really do allow some downtime in our busy lives. Happily, cultivating a taste for tea-taking powerfully encourages us to explore the plentiful and pleasant options which await leisure seekers. It can be tremendous fun to arrange a delectable spread of tea treats when our garden is at its peak of perfection and then to summon our friends to enjoy the two together. It can be equally (or rather more) satisfying to escape to the garden alone, with a pot of hot water and a single cup.

To me, there is an almost erotic pleasure in wandering through the garden early or late, teapot in hand, snipping scented leaves and flowers straight into the pot. I cover them with simmering water and let them brew for a few minutes while I settle myself on a comfortable bench. Finally, I pour out a fragrant cup of homemade tea whose very steam is healing.

The following chapters will explain how to create settings for making and taking tea of various kinds, from the formalities of English afternoon tea or Asian tea ceremonies to the spontaneity of the garden's daily offerings. Happily, this need not be an especially difficult or arduous process. Indeed, it doesn't matter how small your available space or how limited your time and budget. Even

Sharing tea and treats with friends is especially pleasant

when the garden is at its summery best.

if your gardening experience is also modest, by applying the design principles explained in this book, you can create a garden which offers at least one place where you can truly relax and savor your world, alone or in good company.

The kind of practical, simple, yet visually effective garden-making presented in these pages is quickly taking hold among garden designers as well as tea drinkers. On the West Coast, where much of today's exciting garden design originates, one of the strongest regional trends is the renewed emphasis on creating places to be within the garden. This is not just a continuation of the English concept of making garden "rooms," or even about finding new ways to make our gardens into extensions of our homes. The point is to allow ourselves to be in the garden in a deeper, more connected way.

The idea is spreading to other parts of the country as well, aided by the increasing popularity of naturalistic garden design. Enclosing the garden with plants arrayed in what appear to be natural layers creates a welcoming ambience which encourages more active use of the enclosed space. During the 1950s, the concept of using outside spaces like living rooms became very popular, again most notably on the West Coast. Soon, however, barbecue pits, conversation circles, patios, and terraces proliferated all across the country. At that time, the emphasis was more on simply spending time outside than on growing wonderful gardens to balance and support all this hardscape. (The man-made surfaces in a garden, from paths to pergolas, are classed by designers as hardscape, while the plants are considered "infill.")

This hardscape-intensive influence persisted well into the '80s, when perennials began to gain (or rather, regain) popularity. Perhaps as a reaction to the earlier emphasis on hard surfaces, the next wave of gardens was very much about perennials, which are in general rather billowy plants. Some of the best-known plant-based gardens are amazing places which approach museum status, much like the English manor gardens they were modeled upon. While they are wonderful places to see and enjoy plants, like those stately gardens of England, they may also be less than welcoming to a full range of human interactions. If you aren't there to work or admire, you can easily feel out of place.

These days, a new style is emerging which borrows some elements from those formal European gardens but is markedly more naturalistic in planting style. These gardens house plenty of plants, in wondrous array. They also offer a variety of places to be in the garden, so that even a small space can serve several sets of needs. This is a winning combination, and I think we'll all be seeing a lot more of it.

One key to the successful development of a flexible small garden is to combine a simple design with fairly complex plantings. Simple designs tend to be both practical and visually restful, and lend themselves to personal interpretation. They also showcase, rather than overwhelm, our plants. Perhaps most importantly, gardeners with limited design experience will enjoy a higher degree of success when not attempting too much.

Simple design does not have to be boringly basic. A good design combines functionality with clean, meaningful lines. For example, on a recent trip to Portland, Oregon, I visited a wonderful small garden, which was uncluttered in overall design yet packed with delightful details, many of them homemade.

By both front and back doors, pretty pebbled mosaics (set in dry cement, then wet down with a water mister) gave old concrete steps a handsome new look. The snug little vegetable garden was framed with open fencing, along which dwarf fruit trees were neatly espaliered. Each fence post was topped with a fat sculpted fruit, so that even in winter, pears and apples deck the garden walk. (The fruits were molded from a paper packing material, then covered with a thin coating of cement, and painted with thinned house paint—these people are clever.)

The old garage had been converted into a handsome potting shed and greenhouse, which was open to the light on two sides. The owners were busily covering the homely old building's sides with hand-molded "stones" they had made from cement. To do this, real river stones were pressed into sand, then removed, and cement was poured into the cavity. They used a dozen different stones for the instant molds, to produce a variety of shapes and sizes, and tinted each batch of cement in earthy tones to get a range of colors.

The reason these people are such masters of illusion is that they are both interior designers. They design the flow of rooms in homes and offices, developing spaces and detailing walls and windows, doors and entries. They, too, agree that simplicity and strength of line is almost always the most important part of garden design.

Interior design skills translate brilliantly in the garden, especially those concerned with creating visual illusions, which are often an essential ingredient in successful design. Small gardens especially need to create a feeling of spaciousness where quarters are cramped. For example, where a blank wall borders a narrow garden area, setting a non-opening gate and one or two trellis-work archways against it will create an implied extension of space. Cover those arches in climbing vines or roses and the illusion works even better. Best of all, back the arches with tall mirrors to reflect the garden back into itself, and even a tiny space will instantly appear much larger.

Another skill which works well both indoors and out is a knack for creating intimate spaces within larger ones. Reorganizing space this way not only makes a limited area seem greater than it is, but offers us a way to see the garden with fresh eyes. In the Portland garden I visited, a tropical-looking tea hut stands to one side of a small lawn. Raised on tall legs, the tea hut is reached by a flight of broad steps. Inside, a soft couch invites comfortable lounging, while low tables hold teacups and treats. Exotic vines clamber up the sides, surrounding tea-takers in a leafy bower. As you look out over the garden, the scene unfolds enticingly. The elevation allows you to see over the low hedges and fences which divide the inner garden space, so several areas blend in floral profusion.

In the same garden, the roof of the old garage has become a pleasantly green retreat. The flat roof was walled in with six-foot-high panels perforated with large cutout window spaces. These are not glassed in, but the divisions between the windows are draped with vines to create living wallpaper.

Boston ivy (*Parthenocissus tricuspidata*), a rowdy rambler of a vine, has completely clothed the walls in four years. Now, the windows are fringed with a dripping green filigree of foliage. Each spring, the window shapes are clipped out, but by midsummer, the curling tendrils extend again to soften the hard lines.

A wall of Boston ivy

creates ruffled curtains

for empty "windows"

through which the

garden below is framed

like a picture.

AN ENGLISH TEA GARDEN

NOWHERE IS THE ENGLISH GENIUS OF

DOMESTICITY MORE NOTABLY EVIDENT

THAN IN THE FESTIVAL OF AFTERNOON TEA.

THE MERE CHINK OF CUPS AND SAUCERS

TUNES THE MIND TO HAPPY REPOSE.

George Gissing | *The Private Papers of Henry Ryecroft*

In my favorite English novels, the characters are always enjoying afternoon tea in the garden. Sometimes the tea table is set in the shade of a spreading chestnut tree, so far from the house that footmen help the maids carry out the laden trays. Sometimes the guests gather by the sunny lawn in laughing groups, the ladies creating their own shade with silk parasols. Sometimes two lovers meet demurely, chaperoned by kindly aunts. Always, the tea-takers are surrounded with masses of flowers in neat beds or bountiful borders.

When they come to the tea table, the guests enjoy a splendid variety of treats along with China or India tea. They nibble on cress sandwiches and crumpets, rock cakes and plum cake with jam, as well as fruit and biscuits (what we would call cookies). This sumptuous spread is simply called afternoon tea, not high tea, as many people assume. An English high tea is a substantial meal of hearty fare, often including boiled eggs, cheese, and masses of toast and jam. It's designed to satisfy hungry farmers and laborers who, at midafternoon, still have long hours of work ahead of them. Afternoon tea, in contrast, is simply about relaxed pleasure in the company of friends.

In some ways, the convivial elegancies of afternoon tea belong to the past. Few of us have time or leisure to create the cornucopia of plenty which was commonplace when every household had a cook and a maid. Even so, it is easy to update the concept so that we can enjoy the same sense of relaxation and leisure with our friends. After all, the festive quality of such get-togethers depends less on specifics of food and drink than on atmosphere.

To create the kind of ambience which made English afternoon tea an art form, we need to consider the underlying design principles which gave those golden gardens their special glow. Once we identify key design elements, we can adapt them to the smaller spaces (and notable lack of trained staff) which characterize the modern American garden. Just as fancy pastries and tea tarts can be replaced with one or two simpler yet delectably satisfying dishes, those English border plants can be edited down to a choice few which give our gardens both substance and finish.

DESIGN ELEMENTS FOR AN ENGLISH TEA GARDEN

In any kind of English garden, the vital design elements come in pairs. The first are enclosure and structure, followed closely by abundance and control. What these concepts mean in England is not precisely what they will mean to Americans. In England, guidebooks refer to anything under ten acres as a small garden, and fantastic houses like Hidcote are dismissed as "architecturally insignificant." Fortunately, the basic design concepts can be scaled down quite well. Those of us who garden in modest urban or suburban plots can still create delightful gardens, however tiny, which provide a happy sense of comfort and ease.

Enclosure, whether from century-old clipped hedges, stone walls, plain wooden fences or even trelliswork covered in ivy, makes an open garden instantly more inviting. Take a typical front yard, surround that empty expanse of grass with some form of visual barrier, and its sense of place is increased dramatically. Even the simplest form of enclosure immediately defines the garden space, creates visual privacy, and modifies traffic noise.

Structure is often lacking in homemade gardens, where contented plants often count more than design considerations. Structure is generally defined as the hardscape which frames the garden and gives its interior shape and focus. These elements are indeed vital to the garden's flow, particularly paths, which direct both foot and eye. Paths are perhaps the most important design element, for their lines give shape to the garden beds, guide our steps, dictate where we

Enclosure is vital to the sense of place and privacy

which characterize English gardens. In them, gardener and visitor alike

feel that they are in a world apart, a place of retreat and peace.

sit and what we see, and make our progress effortless or awkward. Altering a narrow, cinder block path to a broad and neatly graveled one will make an enormous difference to the look and feel of the garden, at once creating a more formal impression and more secure footing.

However, structure can also come from plants, particularly trees and evergreen shrubs. The trunks of mature trees make living columns which lead the eye upward, connecting to the treeline. (This means the irregular line made by trees against the sky, and usually includes trees throughout the neighborhood as well as your own.) Evergreen shrubs create visual ladders between big-scale elements like tall trees or large buildings and the intimate, human scale of the garden. They also bring a comforting solidity of mass and form to beds full of frothy flowers, most of which lack substance (in a design sense) on their own.

In a very small garden, medium-sized shrubs will fill the role of trees, and compact ones will carry the eye up and ease it back down that visual ladder. Where space is strictly limited, narrow (fastigiate) trees and shrubs provide the desired height without excess girth. Italian cypress (*Cupressus sempervirens* 'Stricta') and skyrocket junipers (*Juniperus virginiana* 'Skyrocket') are classic examples of beautifully textured but skinny hedge trees.

The choice of evergreen shrubs is too enormous to attempt to catalog here, but wherever possible, it's best to try for a good mixture of needled and broadleaf plants. Having only conifers gives a garden a stiff, rather chilly and formal look which is difficult to modify. Even a few broad-leaved evergreens will help to link hard-edged conifers to softer-textured perennials. In the coldest climates, choices are most restricted, since only conifers and a handful of mostly dwarf broadleaf shrubs will survive harsh winters. In USDA zones 4 and 5, the possibilities improve, since we can add certain daphnes, rhododendrons, viburnums, mahonias, and so forth to the list. In zones 6 through 9, an enormous palette of plants can be employed.

To find the best selections for your particular area, visit nurseries, garden centers, and gardens as well as public parks and arboretums. Make special trips in each season, taking notes about which evergreens catch your eye each time. Generally, if a plant looks good in January, it will make a reliable cornerstone for your garden composition. Over time, you can assemble a selection of shapely trees and shrubs which offer beauties in every season. If the garden is small, you will need to edit out less worthy plants as choicer ones become available. Over time, the thoughtful addition of appropriate evergreen plants will simply increase the sense of abundance.

Abundance is an essential quality of English gardens. Though beds and borders are primly edged and scrupulously maintained, the plantings within them are ebullient and joyful. Generous clumps and sweeps of each kind of plant are arrayed in colorful combinations which shift with the seasons. In small gardens, the sweeps are scaled down to clusters, and a single potently shaped plant may well be plenty. Certain plants, like catmints (*Nepeta*) or lavenders, may be used many times along the border's edge. This creates visual continuity, uniting a variety of plant forms and colors through moderate repetition. The key is balance: too much of anything is boring, while too little may look insignificant. Finding the balance involves trial and error, experimenting with quantities and

In English gardens, good design dictates a delicate balance between structure and abundance.

Plants are often generously arrayed within formal beds, so that their informality of shape

is countered by the firm lines of path and hedge or wall.

colors until your eye is delighted. Keeping the balance involves editing, because plant communities change over time, just as human ones do.

Mixed borders, combinations of woody and perennial plants, are among the most stable plant communities if well planned. Backed with border shrubs such as hydrangeas, shrub roses, and foaming spiraeas, they bubble over with blossom from spring into fall. Perennials are tucked about the skirts of the shrubs, which are in turn sheltered by the trees that mark the garden's perimeter. The beds are as full as good culture permits, so that by the end of May, no bare soil can be seen. Plants overlap in living mulch which conserves soil moisture and shades out young weeds.

Although abundance is achieved by accentuating the natural bounty of our plants, it is balanced by control. In English gardens, keeping the balance is very much about the dominance of nature. Historically, this concept underlies most European garden design, from the medieval monastic herb gardens to the stately showplaces of the past century. Traditional formalism demands not only symmetry in planting but a rigid perfectionism in maintenance. Most American gardeners prefer to emulate the looser, more naturalistic look of the modern plantings at Sissinghurst and Great Dixter.

In these famous gardens, great experimental gardeners (Vita Sackville-West and Christopher Lloyd) have explored the art of dynamic, living balance. Ideally, plants are placed where their natural shape and size are precisely what is wanted. At best, control is reduced to good care, rather than the sometimes savage intervention required by less thoughtful planting. This kind of control means allowing plants their freedom, but also implies an inner balance, not allowing thugs to overcome less robust companions. The gardener's job is that of a peace-keeper, making sure everybody has enough but nobody (like gorgeous but greedy roses) takes too much.

PLANT PORTRAITS | *Choosing Plants for an English Tea Garden*

A good-sized English garden may hold hundreds, if not thousands, of plants. Honing the list down to just a few is difficult, so begin with your favorites. In my case, I always want something fragrant in bloom, so I seek out sweet-scented plants from nurseries which specialize in perfumed plants. I also consult my nose when shopping, giving preference to plants which smell delectable. Since many sweeties also taste terrific, many are right at home in a tea garden.

I also want color for as long as possible, so I shop early and late, cruising nurseries and garden centers all year long. Monthly observation trips keep gardeners awake to seasonal bests in their regions. To keep your tea garden plantings visually coherent, develop a color theme. This can be as simple or complex as you like. White gardens mingle white flowers with silver, gray, and often blue foliage plants for a sophisticated look. For a richer look, combine rose and pink with purple and lavender. If you prefer a cheerful, sunny effect, mix yellow, blue, and orange flowers in every possible shade and tint. When you shop, keep your palette in mind and your new purchases will fit readily amongst the established plantings.

A few outstanding plants earn a place both for beauty and for what they bring to the teapot. Any English garden worth the label is bound to have

Repetition of key plants helps to keep color themes coherent. Contrasting upright, spiky forms with rounded mounds creates more stimulating contours in billowy beds and borders.

roses, lavender, and a clambering hops vine. Here are some guidelines for selecting those which will perform double duty in a tea garden, adding both long-term beauty to the borders and a delicious presence in the pot.

LAVENDER

English lavender smells and tastes like the essence of summer, combining a Mediterranean warmth with English crispness. A single leaf or two adds depth of flavor and scintillating scent to herbal teas. The penetrating aroma of lavender has for centuries been considered a sure cure for grief and a comfort for a sore heart. *Lavandula vera* is the old medicinal form used in home-brewed remedies, but for tea, any good garden form will do nicely. Classic English garden plants include tidy little *L. angustifolia* 'Munstead', with green leaves and sea blue flowers, or the slightly smaller 'Hidcote', gray of leaf and dusty purple in bloom. In cold climates, grow lavenders in pots to set about your seating area. In winter, shelter them in a garage or basement until killing frosts are past. Elsewhere, use silvery, evergreen lavenders as bed edgers, creating a ruffled row of blue flowers whose sparkling scent will make your tea parties feel utterly authentic.

ROSES

No English garden is complete without roses, whether they be hybrid teas lined out in precise rows or climbers tumbling in wild swags over walls or out of trees. For tea purposes, almost any kind will do. A few petals of a fragrant rose will turn ordinary black tea into drinkable potpourri, while the plump hips add a booster dose of vitamin C as well as delicious sweetness to the pot. Those who prefer to spend their time sipping tea rather than spraying nasty chemicals will seek out healthy, hardy, carefree roses for their tea gardens. Among the very best (and hardiest) are rugosa roses, beautiful toughs which take drought and sun in stride, providing several months of bloom and masses of hips in exchange for decent soil and ordinary care.

Many species of roses are easy to grow well, and quite a few offer great hips as well as lovely, fragrant flowers. My favorites include the spring-blooming *Rosa primula,* whose dainty yellow, single blossoms smother the branches for weeks. *R. glauca* is a colorist's dream, with pewtery purple foliage and hot red hips. Its soft pink, single flowers are charming rather than showy, but this is one of the few roses that can hold its own for overall good looks in a mixed border.

GOLDEN HOPS

Vines lend a look of luxuriance to gardens, and hops will do it in a hurry. Trained across an arbor or pergola, hops vines will create pleasant shade for a midsummer tea party in a single season. Hardy to zone 3, common hops (*Humulus lupulus*) has large, lobed leaves on bristly stems which twist themselves purposefully up anything standing still. The golden form, 'Aurea', is a quintessential English garden plant whose old gold foliage looks especially lustrous in partial or dappled shade.

Female plants drip with long, decorative bracts in which the tiny flowers nestle. Stuffed into sachets and tucked under pillows, these bracts are supposed to deliver sweet dreams. In the teapot, a handful of hops bracts adds the scent of new-mown hay and a slightly musty pungency. This herb is considered highly soothing to rattled nerves.

A JAPANESE TEA GARDEN

I CONSIDER HOW EASY IT IS TO BE CONTENT

WITH A SMALL SPACE. EVERY DAY, I STROLL

IN THE GARDEN FOR PLEASURE. . . . AND WALK

AROUND MY LONELY PINE TREE, STROKING IT.

Tao Yuanming | *Fourth-Century Poet*

The tea ceremony which arose some five hundred years ago in Japan had a revolutionary effect on garden design, and continues to influence the way gardens are made and experienced to this day. In those early days, Japanese gardens were heavily influenced by Chinese garden styles as well as by the Chinese Buddhist philosophy and practice which evolved in Japan into Zen.

Over time, Japanese Zen philosophers and garden-makers created distinctive styles which varied considerably from those earlier models. In the mid-sixteenth century, one of the most important Zen tea masters, Sen No Rikyu, developed what remains the quintessential school of tea garden design. Called the *roji* or dewy path garden, this style represented the meeting place of art and philosophy, which were held to be the highest possible pursuits for the educated classes.

The tea garden was also a place in which people were made constantly aware of their interconnectedness with the natural world. Because so many of the tea garden's architectural elements (and even plant selection and placement) are highly symbolic, it is easy to overlook or misunderstand the importance of this vital design component. To Western eyes, many Japanese gardens look extremely contrived, reminding us more of the artificial than the natural. To a culture steeped in literary and spiritual allusion, however, every object and plant carries an illustrious heritage of meaning, so that the idea of the natural world is evoked. The placement of each garden item is equally weighted with historical associations and references which are not apparent to casual observation.

The way each garden sits within its site and relative to its overall setting is also fraught with symbolism which conveys a complex series of concepts to the educated viewer. In one sense, the whole message is very simple: the link between humans and nature is as much spiritual as physical, and the role of the tea garden was (and is) to open the eyes of highly acculturated, sophisticated people to the profound depth and essential simplicity of that relationship.

Eventually, the roji tea garden became an idealized retreat from the difficulties and cares of daily life, a concept as welcome today as it was centuries ago. The model roji tea garden was itself small, and contained a snug little hut which was often scarcely a yard square inside. Here, four or five friends could gather (kneeling on tatami mats) to take tea and exchange views on art, poetry, music, and philosophy. Worldly or political discussions were strictly discouraged, and the emphasis was on contemplative thoughtfulness.

Before approaching this inner sanctum, tea-takers prepared themselves by strolling down a narrow path, which often zigzagged through a courtyard, in order to ceremonially leave the world behind. The wandering line of the path was intended to confuse any pursuing wicked spirits which might try to hinder those seeking higher development. The path itself usually incorporated some stepping stones, which created a further conceptual separation between the outer and inner worlds.

Stone lanterns would light the way at night or on foggy evenings, and also represented the illumination of spirit which guides those who seek enlightenment. Guests would pause outside the hut, where a tiny waiting area held a stone basin of water. This miniature garden "room" was a place for additional reflection and purification. Tea participants could wash their hands or sip a cup of water before entering the hut, symbolically rinsing away worldly thoughts and problems.

The colors of a Japanese garden herald the changing of the seasons.

Fallen leaves from a cherry tree celebrate the intensity of autumn.

DESIGN ELEMENTS FOR A JAPANESE TEA GARDEN

Few of us can hope to recreate a truly authentic Japanese tea garden, yet we can apply the basic principles to our own setting and situation. By adapting core design concepts and components appropriately, we can make a successfully meditative tea garden almost anywhere. How we do this will depend on the space, time, and materials available; what matters most about the result is that it works for us.

There is a delightful story about a famous (and very well-funded) Japanese tea garden in North America which opened a few years ago. A group of Japanese garden designers came to see it and toured the whole place with great interest. When asked what they thought, they all bowed solemnly, and the eldest one said politely, "It is very beautiful. We have nothing like it in our country."

The lesson here is probably that less is more. Fortunately, too, the result of our efforts need not be perfectly realistic or correct in every detail in order to achieve the desired atmosphere. All that is necessary is that the elements of our design combine to create a genuine retreat from the daily fret and toil of the workaday world. Best of all, we can quite authentically make an effective tea garden when we are limited to a tiny area. It is impossible to construct an English border or cottage garden in a postage stamp yard or on a condo balcony, but making a viable tea garden may be quite possible in either spot. Perhaps the greatest gift those ancient tea masters offer to modern garden-makers is the understanding that no space is too small to become a contemplative retreat.

Although the Asian tea gardens originated on the other side of the world and many centuries before the classic English gardens, they rely on intriguingly similar design principles. Here again, enclosure is imperative. To make a tea garden, we must create a visual and physical enclosure. Only by blocking out the world (at least symbolically) can we create an effective retreat.

The heart of the Zen tea garden is the tea hut. This can be any form of enclosed space with a roof and at least two walls to shelter the occupant from weather. Not many North Americans are truly comfortable kneeling on mats, but a roofed viewing platform big enough to hold a single chair (or perhaps a companionable pair) will suffice. Where permanent walls are difficult to construct, rolled bamboo window blinds (perhaps backed by less attractive but more solid ones) make adequate barriers to wind and rain. Once shelter is achieved, it is deeply satisfying to watch and listen to the rain or snow while sipping a steaming cup of tea. Observing nature closely without being at the mercy of the elements is part of the charm of the situation.

To reach that inner sanctum, we need a pathway. If possible, it should lead us away from the house in an indirect manner, passing though a gate or entry into a courtyard (again enclosed) before approaching the tea hut. Where space permits, the path may flow like water, making a symbolic river which pours past the plants. Plain sheets of gravel may be periodically broken with casually grouped beach stones to suggest a meandering river bed. Pebbled paving stones or patterned beach stones set into concrete also work well.

Grass or moss can serve the same purpose, but because moss wears poorly underfoot, some of those symbolic stepping stones will help preserve its vitality and appearance. Where space is extremely limited, even a single stepping stone

Even where garden space is restricted to a tiny corner,

a contemplative tea retreat may still be contrived.

In an apartment or condo, a trellised retreat might be

created on a deck or patio.

can represent the wandering pathway of the roji. A low wall, trellis panels, bamboo fencing, or any other visual baffle will create the necessary division between the outer and inner worlds.

The inner courtyard which the path traverses may be spacious and serene, though if necessary, it might be a mere yard across and still function as a conceptual separation. In truly tight quarters, a miniature version could be contained in the sort of rugged stone trough used to house alpine plants. Such stone containers also make splendid water basins for the ceremonial washing, as do carved stone bowls. If both are unavailable, a rough-hewn wooden trough or bowl can be substituted.

Room must be found for the stone lantern as well, which may be functional or simply decorative. Some lanterns are fitted with interior holders for candles or lamp oil, while others are built to burn the traditional lantern fuel, which is the dried pith of a lanky shrub called *Kerria japonica*. This shaggy creature has long, arching arms that are covered in spring with sunny flowers that look exactly like dandelions. Not compact or tidy enough for placement within a tea garden, kerria might easily be grown in the alley or by the compost bin, where year-round good looks are less critical.

The next necessary ingredient is a view. If no fabulous sight of distant mountains or water happens to present itself, the garden-maker must create an inner view. Very frequently, this consists of a planted area, again enclosed with low walls. If large trees surround the tea hut, a traditional planting would include masses of moss flowing across the forest floor, interrupted only by gnarled tree roots, a few ferns, and an unusual rock. In a sunny, open site, the centerpiece of an interior view might be a striking specimen tree, perhaps a multi-trunked Japanese maple, a weeping 'Red Jade' crabapple, or a lone pine, preferably bent and twisted with age.

An abundance of trees should also frame the garden if at all possible. Most often, this is accomplished through *shakkei*, or borrowed views, an important Asian design principle. What this means is organizing sight lines, using screening and various visual baffles to direct the attention beyond the garden to include distant views. We can also borrow trees from the whole neighborhood, using the treeline (what we see against the sky) of surrounding properties to create a second or third tier of enclosure for our inner garden.

When we drop out distracting objects like cars, buildings, and satellite disks by screening them from view, what's left is often richly layered and majestic in scale. Suddenly, the busy street is gone, and the garden seems embowered in mature, luxuriant trees. Sometimes this illusion is only effective from certain angles, but if it holds for the person seated in the tea hut, that's all the magic you need.

PLANT PORTRAITS | *Choosing Plants for a Japanese Tea Garden*

Meditative and subtle in effect, Asian-influenced tea garden plantings are sparse yet not necessarily austere. Indeed, many of them offer a continual, if understated, display of color and interest all year. The emphasis on showcasing specimen plants with pronounced character, or *shibui,* gives these gardens an architectural quality often lacking in billowing borders.

Though the classic tea garden plant palette is generally quite limited, like the design elements, this is also subject to interpretation. In most Asian garden

The interplay of a geometric granite pathway and a resplendent maple

lend strength and serenity to this Japanese garden design.

styles, plants are chosen as much for their literary or traditional associations as for visual effect. Thus, every garden will hold bamboo and pines, bananas and plums, all of which have multiple symbolic meanings.

Though Asia abounds with an astonishingly rich flora, very few of the collector's treasures prized in England and North America are cultivated. A few roses, especially ancient hybrid forms of Chinese species such as 'Old Blush' (also called the 'Monthly Rose') may be found in tea gardens. On the whole, however, sculptural plants with strong lines are favored over those with fabulous flowers.

Indeed, rather than the abundance of the English borders, Asian tea masters strove to achieve a careful concert of elements. In each meticulous composition, plants and objects such as ornamental rocks or stone lanterns are given equal value. Both are placed with thoughtful deliberation, seeking always to create an environment which is spare and spacious rather than ornate or billowy.

In the open courtyard and path areas, a few azaleas or small rhododendrons give the tea garden year-round presence. Traditionally, the rhododendrons would be dwarf forms which grow extremely slowly. The azaleas would be sheared tightly to resemble smooth stones. These days, many people prefer a looser, more natural appearance, and would instead select choice plants with a naturally tidy shape and restrained habit.

By choosing compact border rhododendrons which have especially attractive foliage, we can provide more lasting interest than when we select them solely for their few weeks of spring color. Instead of buying ordinary border rhododendrons, look for the charming yaks, hybrids of *Rhododendron yakushimanum*

Asian maiden grasses
like Miscanthus
sinensis 'Morning
Light' remain graceful
for most of the year,
while any wandering
breeze awakens their
musical rustling.

which have enticingly felted foliage in silver, fawn, or rust. Most have pink or creamy flowers as well, but are especially prized for their lovely evergreen leaves. Many of the new yaks are hardy even in cold winter areas, and with some shelter from wind and hard frost, they remain attractive all year.

Azaleas, too, can be selected for foliage as much as for flower. Though most are deciduous, they frequently offer a bonus of vibrant fall color. If we buy them in autumn, when many azaleas display brilliant sunset tints, we can choose those which offer splendid coloration in two seasons. When azaleas are well grown, their gay blaze brightens the autumn garden for weeks, usually lasting far longer than the fleeting flowers of spring.

Shady gardens nestled beneath mature trees may need very little planting. Often, thoughtful editing of natural woodlands yields more pleasing compositions than introducing exotic border beauties. Mossy paths, ferns, and a few choice woodlanders will provide all that is wanted. If structural shrubs are needed, lily of the valley shrub, *Pieris* x 'Flame of the Forest', boasts clustered spring flowers as well as evergreen foliage which undergoes four distinct color changes over the course of the year. Mountain laurel (*Kalmia* sp.) also looks at home in such settings. For an exotic look, *Fatsia japonica,* with its long-fingered leaves, or a fuzzy stemmed sumac will contrast potently with the rounded canopies of Japanese maples or upright katsuras.

Classic tea gardens would certainly have the famous trio so necessary to Chinese gardens and so frequently found in Japanese gardens as well. Called the three friends of winter, they are pine, bamboo, and winter plum. A solitary, evergreen pine is the heart of many tea gardens. Picturesquely gnarled and bent with age (or by means of large-scale bonsai techniques), the pine represents the lasting strengths of maturity, the power of virtue to survive despite time and trouble, and the endlessly recycling nature of eternity. In a large garden, a great, mature pine could shelter the tea hut. In a tiny garden, a miniature bonsai pine grown in a lovely container might be the centerpiece of the constructed interior view.

Bamboo, also evergreen, succeeds because of its flexibility, bending beneath the snow and wind rather than breaking. Pliant wands of bamboo symbolize resilience in the face of adversity and the suppleness of the free mind. In larger gardens, running bamboos can form living walls to screen views and redirect sight lines. Elsewhere, these relentless travelers are best contained in sturdy pots set on tiles to prevent their errant roots from escaping through the drain holes. In very small gardens, dwarf bamboos may be most suitable, though big specimens in pots look exceedingly elegant and dramatic. Where winters are fierce, bamboos will need to be protected from severe frosts, so container-grown plants will prove most practical. In very cold settings, large grasses may be substituted for bamboos, providing a similar silhouette and shape and the same satisfying rustle in the wind.

The plum referred to in this context is invariably *Prunus mume*, the winter-flowering plum which opens its delicate flowers even in the snow. Winter plum stands for hope, rebirth, and the triumph of spring over winter. Only hardy to zone 8, *Prunus mume* will be most successful in the south and along the West Coast, where it will grow in sheltered spots as far north as British Columbia. Elsewhere, it can be replaced with any early flowering shrubby plum or cherry, of which numerous lovely and hardy forms abound.

AN HERBAL TEA GARDEN

PEPPERMINT, HOREHOUND, AND TARRAGON; SESAME, CARAWAY,

ANISE; LAVENDER, ROSEMARY, RUE; PEONY, SWEET MARJORAM,

AND THYME—THEIR FLAVOR AND FRAGRANCE AGAIN CARRY

ROMANCE, MYSTERY, LEGENDS, AND MAGIC, LIFTING US OUT OF

THE HURRYING PRESENT, EVEN IF JUST FOR A LITTLE WHILE.

Rosetta Clarkson | *Magic Gardens*

The classic herb garden, where medicinal and culinary plants are arranged in tidy geometrical patterns, has roots as old as agriculture and far older than geometry. Five thousand years ago, Chinese physicians gathered and grew a multitude of herbs to cure ills of body, mind, and spirit. Four thousand years ago, Egyptian healers used fragrant herbs from special gardens to cleanse, heal, and refresh the sick and to embalm the dead. Three thousand years ago, the Greek healer Hippocrates created the roots of modern medicine, growing dozens of Mediterranean native plants for their medicinal properties. Two thousand years ago, Roman matriarchs cultivated healing herbs in well-organized kitchen gardens. A thousand years ago, nuns and monks in medieval monasteries tended physic gardens and concocted herbal simples in order to heal their ailing neighbors.

The societal value of herbal gardens waned as Western medicine gained status, yet the healing herbs have remained in continuous cultivation. Country women far from medical assistance still tucked a few plants of boneset (*Eupatorium perfoliatum*) and woundwort (St. John's wort, or *Hypericum calycinum*) in with the kitchen and household herbs. Many of these last did double duty: rosemary soothed a cough, relieved asthma, and sweetened bad breath as well as sweetening the contents of the linen closet. Lavender made a cleansing astringent, while basilicum powder was packed into wounds.

Well into the nineteenth century, many houses in England, Europe, and America contained a still room, where the mistress of the house concocted tonics and tinctures, extracts and essential oils. Their herb gardens held the same mixture of all-purpose herbs and herbal simples (plants with one sovereign virtue) that characterized the medieval physic gardens. Lemon balm and basil, tarragon and tansy, dill and fennel, coriander and chervil all combined with poppies and roses, or lilies and bellflowers to make those highly practical gardens both fragrant and beautiful.

Beauty, however, was a less important principle in the design of the healing herb garden than order. Only over the past century have the subtle beauties and shapes of the healing herbs been valued for their ornamental qualities. In this century, influential English gardeners such as Gertrude Jekyll and Vita Sackville-West started trends for incorporating herbs like silvery artemisia, purple sage, and fragrant lavender into colorist borders. This created such a demand for especially attractive forms that today we can draw upon an exceptionally broad palette of choice plants when we decide to design our own herbal tea gardens.

DESIGN ELEMENTS FOR AN HERBAL TEA GARDEN

Over the past five or six decades, a great revival of interest in herbal lore and practices has caused thousands of modern herb gardens to be made. In England, most repeat the traditional planting patterns which date back to the Middle Ages. As a glimpse through any classic herbal will show you, these consist largely of wide paths in straight lines surrounded by symmetrical beds. In them, the herbs are planted in solid blocks or masses, grouped according to kind and color as well as size and cultural needs.

In these highly practical gardens, the beds may be rectangular, square, triangular, or semicircular, but they are generally clean and simple in line. All radiate from or cluster around some central object, which might be a fruit tree, a bee skep, or a sundial. Since Elizabethan days, the herb garden sundial has invariably been underplanted with thyme, to perpetuate the classic herbal pun. Elizabethans were also fond of sundials which bore the inscription, "I count only the sunny hours." They were a lot more cheerful than the lugubrious Victorians, who preferred the rather sinister, "It's later than you think."

Modern border perennials and ancient herbal remedies share common ground

in these bright beds. Many plants we now grow simply for floral beauty

were prized by our ancestors for their healing ways.

In ancient herb gardens, a well head or fountain was another popular center-piece. Though garden wells are far less common today, small recirculating fountains are readily available and can easily be installed by amateurs. In modern herb gardens, a handsome water jar, a statue, or a large container full of plants often occupies this central spot.

All over Europe, the traditional shape for the herb garden was a long rectangle, facing south and backed by a wall of brick or stone. The more tender herbs and fruit trees such as apricots and figs were placed near the wall to encourage full ripening of fruit and the development of essential oils in the herb foliage. Indeed, the entire herb garden, like the kitchen garden, was invariably enclosed by walls or some combination of hedge and wall. Long ago, garden enclosure was not a design principle but vital fortification, intended to protect food and medicines from human enemies as well as roaming animals which might browse destructively amid the herbs. Indeed, the very word *garden* has ancient roots from *garth* and *gart*—which mean "an enclosed space."

Enclosure remains important for English herb gardens, where the shelter of a warm brick wall helps ripen Mediterranean herbs which might otherwise sulk in cool, sunless summers. In colonial America, where sun was plentiful but labor and materials were scarce, brick walls were replaced with split rail fences or low hedges. As settlements grew less rugged and more sophisticated, these enclosing hedges were often replaced by interwoven fruit trees, pruned and trained as a flat, espalier fence. Like the medieval physic gardens, colonial herb gardens combined utter practicality with simplicity of design and planting.

In vivid contrast stands the knot garden, a European design conceit in which herbs were arranged in elaborate patterns. This concept dates back some three thousand years B.C., to the Sumerians, though similar motifs are also found in ancient Celtic, Roman, and Islamic art. In early European adaptations, knot gardens imitated actual knots, with rowed plants interlacing over and through each other exactly as rope would. Only two or three kinds of herbs were used, so the effect was of foliar ribbons running through beds framed with clipped thyme or hyssop.

By the sixteenth century, knot gardens were all the rage in Europe and England, where two distinct types emerged. Open knot gardens were quartered into four symmetrical beds, each filled with herbs in running patterns, the spaces between filled with summer flowers. Open knot gardens were preferred by those who wanted to walk amongst their herbs and enjoy their scents close at hand. Closed knot gardens, which had no interior paths, were best viewed from above, whether from a high terrace or an interior window. Their patterns became madly baroque as garden designers vied to create ever more astonishing variations on an endless form. Soon, the literalism which dictated early knot garden patterns gave way to more fanciful interpretations. The most admired closed knot gardens were laced with writhing, gyrating lines which were torturous to plant and tend. The filling of the ornate knots might well contain herbs, but could also involve practically anything from flowering plants to colored clay or pebbles, bits of bone, or pieces of metal.

By the eighteenth century, the term *knot garden* had come to mean a square garden "room" enclosed by walls and inset with strictly quartered beds edged with trimmed boxwood and filled with intricately patterned plantings. Ironically, this

Dwarf fruit trees may be pruned into espaliered walls to create garden "rooms" within a larger space. This charming example proves that simple planting can be both practical and visually appealing.

might be a design recipe for the now-classic English herb garden, so long as the intricate plantings were replaced with patterns of elegant simplicity.

PLANT PORTRAITS | *Choosing Plants for an Herbal Tea Garden*

The healing garden is a peaceful haven, full of herbs for making tonics and toners, from ginseng and licorice to mints and mustard. In it, the gardener can concoct and savor traditional European tisanes of rose hips or sage and fennel, sweetened with herbal honey and artichoke extract. In summer, such a garden will be alive with bees and hummingbirds, for though few herb flowers are showy to human eyes, they are madly attractive to pollinators. Even in winter, the healing garden is not an empty place, for shrubby, evergreen herbs like pillar rosemary (*Rosmarinus officinalis* 'Tuscan Blue') remain fully clothed and handsome, while many others leave resting rosettes (as well as a haunting hint of summer fragrance) to mark their homes.

The uncluttered lines and pleasing proportions of the classic herb garden make it a relaxing place to sit in any season, so it's a good idea to site a bench in a spot where you also want luxuriant evergreen herbs. That way, you'll be able to enjoy the pungent aromas even in the off seasons, and their strong shapes will provide structure for the quiet garden. Sweet bay, sage, and lavender all hold their looks year-round, except in the coldest climates. In such places, we do well to copy a medieval idea and grow tender herbs in large pots, which can sit beside the bench all summer, then be stored in the house or a greenhouse all winter. In medieval times, pots of herbs were placed within the beds as well as on gravel or flagged terraces. If we confine running herbs like mints and comfrey in oversized pots, they can be safely placed in the smallest gardens, where their thuggish ways might otherwise forbid them entry. What's more, the added height and sleek lines of handsome ornamental pots will help break up the tussocky-hummocky outlines of beds which hold a lot of low growers like thyme and oregano and chives.

No matter what style we choose, the first requirement for a successful herb garden is sunshine. A great majority of healing tea herbs grow best in full sun and well-drained soil. Before we begin to think about plans and patterns, we must make sure we can offer our herbs the setting they need in order to flourish. If only partial sun is possible, we will need to choose herb species and varieties that tolerate shade, such as sweet woodruff, bugbane (*Cimicifuga*), angelica, sweet cecily, bee balm (*Monarda*), boneset (*Eupatorium perfoliatum*), lovage, golden feverfew, and hyssop.

Unless we take these vital factors into consideration from the very beginning, the most attractive design in the world will not succeed. The key to any good garden design is happy plants. If the plants look great, the garden looks great. If the plants are leggy and tumbling, sprawling all over each other while trying to reach the sun, or if they are parched and withered, wishing desperately for a little shade, the overall effect is definitely one of unease, no matter how beautiful the lines of paths and beds and walls might be.

Those ancient physic gardens held dozens of contented plants, invariably arranged in neat patterns. Usually, healing herbs were grouped according to their care and culture, with sun lovers divided from those that craved water.

In autumn months and cooler climes,

tea herbs often appreciate the reflected heat of a warm wall.

This is still an excellent idea, and your herbs will thank you for adapting it. In many monasteries, the plants were further clustered according to purpose. Deadlier nightshades, foxgloves, and mandrake would be segregated safely away from the kitchen herbs. Plants like sage or horehound, which had multiple medicinal virtues as well as culinary ones, might appear in several places. Those which were in constant use, such as fragrant strewing herbs (laid thickly on floors to sweeten the indoor rooms), common remedies, and kitchen favorites, were naturally planted in quantity. Bulk herbs were usually grown in solid blocks or rows, but sometimes they were in simple decorative patterns. A low row of shaggy gray santolina might hide the bare knees of a taller hedgerow of lavender, in turn backed by groups of tall white Madonna lilies, shrub roses, towering cardoons or artichokes, and enormous, angel-winged angelicas. Such a composition would have a great deal of presence, though visual effect (other than tidiness) was rarely even a consideration.

While modern herb gardens tend to be subtle rather than brilliant, relying more on textural contrasts than any effulgence of flower, medieval herb gardens were far brighter places. Roses and lilies, peonies and honeysuckle were prized for their place in the medieval pharmacopoeia, as were angelica, valerian, lavender, catmint, and many plants we grow today purely for their ornamental contribution. A surprising number of modern border plants, from perennials to shrubs, bulbs, vines, and ground covers, found homes in the European physic gardens.

In our modern healing gardens, enclosure can come from fences if we have no walls, but we can also create green architecture quite quickly. Set a row of espaliered fruit trees at right angles to an existing hedge for two sides. The others can be enclosed by large herbs, from pokeweed (*Phytolacca americana*) to bronze fennel, angelica, and lovage. In healing gardens, the softness of living walls can provide an important part of their charm. Edging can be carried out with a variety of compact herbs, from teucrium to hyssop, bushy thymes, and santolinas, while low interior hedges can be made with sages, lavenders, and rosemary. At the path's edge and near seating, large perennials like feverfew, wormwood, lemon balm, and clary sages will provide a delightful balance of sweet, brisk, pungent, and aromatic scents, creating an ever-altering, living perfume which is as healing as the teas we brew.

SAGE AND ARTEMISIA

Plants of wisdom and healing, sages and artemisias are sacred to Artemis, moon goddess and early feminist. Like their namesake, these plants have a cool, silvery beauty and great strength of character. Both do well in sunny, well-drained soil, with little or no supplementary water in summer.

Artemisias are usually represented by southernwood, *Artemisia abrontanum,* which was used for a great variety of troubles. It makes a tall, lusty shrub with lacy, gray foliage that scents the entire garden. Their bitter lemon flavor is pleasantly astringent in teas if used sparingly, and the dried foliage adds a delicious scent to the linen closet, where it will repel moths. Wormwood, *A. absinthium,* was used to make the soporific (and addictive) liqueur absinthe and to ease coughs in tea or syrup. Its beautiful form, 'Lambrook Silver', is especially good for dried arrangements or herb craft, and a single leaf will add an invigorating quality to tonic teas without harm.

Sun is the first requirement for many tea herbs.

Ranked in their shaggy rows, they revel in heat and light.

Culinary sage, *Salvia officinalis,* comes in several colors and forms, from the great, silvery leaves of 'Holt's Mammoth' to the dusky purple of 'Purpurascens', or the lemon-lime of 'Icterina'. All are semi-evergreen, low-growing shrubs in mild climates, and all grow very nicely in containers if need be. They make excellent anchors for the ends of rows, or flank a bench with grace and dignity. A few leaves add a delicious depth to rich, savory tea blends, especially when combined with lemon thyme and rosemary.

HOREHOUND

This quietly beautiful family of plants includes several related plants, all of them good looking and easy to grow. White horehound, *Marrubium vulgare,* is a native Mediterranean healing herb grown since prehistoric times to treat a catalog of woes, from regulating women's cycles to staunching and cleansing wounds. Horehound tea is still considered a reliable appetite stimulant and tummy settler for invalids and children, while stronger brews are used to calm persistent coughs. Its gray-green foliage, rounded and faintly fuzzy, smells wonderful after rain or on warm, sunny days. This is the one to choose for the tea garden, for a few leaves added to a pot of fresh herbs will make an intriguingly rich-tasting brew. Lean, sandy soil and full sun will produce the best plants.

Black horehound, *Ballota nigra,* looks similar but has a rather rank smell and decided takeover tendencies. If you get this one, put it in a pot, for it is attractive, but set it where nobody will brush against the leaves and keep it out of the teapot, for both its flavor and medicinal properties are too strong for comfort.

ARTICHOKE

Strikingly architectural in form, artichokes and the closely related cardoons bring majestic bulk and dramatic form to the garden. In 1633, John Gerard advised in his *Herbal* that artichokes be given "fat and fruitful" soil, adding that "they do love water and moist ground." He points out that "they commit great error who cut away to side or superfluous leaves," thinking to gain greater yields, since those long leaves funnel water closer to the thirsty roots. His advice remains good, for anybody wanting to enjoy the beauty of artichokes or cardoons should give them a rich spot and plenty of room to spread out those big leaves, as well as ample water.

In Gerard's day, artichokes were appreciated at the table, but the young buds, steeped in wine, were also considered an effective aphrodisiac, while artichoke hearts, boiled in wine, improved body odor. Monastic gardeners probably grew them for their mild diuretic qualities, though it was also said that eating artichokes prevented sexual incontinence. In tea gardens, artichokes serve as natural sweeteners, for they have the unusual property of making anything you eat or drink with them taste intensely sweet. The tough, outer leaves of artichoke buds can be used fresh or frozen (they don't dry especially well) to impart sweetness to tea blends.

A COTTAGE TEA GARDEN

IN EVERY VILLAGE AND HAMLET IN THE LAND

THERE WERE THESE LITTLE GARDENS, ALWAYS GAY

AND NEVER GARISH, AND SO OBVIOUSLY LOVED

Margery Fish | *The Cottage Garden*

While the stately homes of England gave rise to overflowing herbaceous borders, the cottages of working folks were surrounded with smaller gardens which combined beauty and practicality in equal measure. Where estates offered room for a dozen specific kinds of garden, cottagers had to fit fruit and flowers, vegetables and herbs into the modest spaces about their more humble homes. Though compact in size and informal in design, these gardens were extremely efficient. Far from being the artless jumble represented by poor imitations, true cottage gardens embodied a concept we think of as very modern; that of "right plant, right place."

Careful attention was paid to proper placement of each plant, giving each precisely what it required to perform optimally. No space was wasted, including verticals. Both house and garden walls were always pressed into service, especially the warm, south-facing ones. Apricot and peach trees would be trained out in trim espaliers so that each succulent fruit could ripen properly. Grapevines and hops were draped on arbors or given the comforting warmth of a wall in order that they too might best provide raw material for winter festivities.

Both home-brewing and wine-making were popular cottage garden pursuits which involved an astonishing array of plants. Elderberry, parsnip, dandelion, and primrose wines were favored by ladies, while men preferred beer and shandy (a mixture of beer and lemonade). Herbs and flowers were also brewed into medicinal teas and tonics for all sorts of ailments, from aching joints to sore hearts. The plants which fulfilled all these roles grew happily cheek to cheek with the family food supply, while every remaining chink of space was filled with flowers.

Indeed, cottage gardens sometimes were referred to as Chinese puzzles for the complexity of their inner arrangements. Madonna lilies might arise between great cabbages, while peonies could be underplanted with parsnips. If plant relationships were informal, they were deeply pragmatic, and the plantings were scrupulously tidy and well kept. Cottage garden paths were direct and utterly workmanlike and there were no design frills whatever, yet the overall effect was both charming and artful. The combination of abundance and control echoed the design principles underlying those lavish estate gardens, though adapted more for function than for style.

Despite being so snugly planted, cottage gardens were full of healthy and exceptionally well-grown plants. Indeed, their excellence was often the despair of the "big house" (cottage folk nearly all worked for landed gentry), where a large staff and ample budgets could not rival the potent effects of loving attention. In the heyday of county fairs and flower shows, cottagers invariably bagged all the blue ribbons for size and quality from under the noses of the wealthy.

Vita Sackville-West speculated that the cottagers' success was due to their habit of tossing family wash water on the beds (for water, too, was a scarce commodity which had to be hauled to the garden by hand). The soapy residues, she thought, might control aphids and other pests, which for some reason never bothered the jam-packed cottage gardens, while the estate gardens were frequently under attack. It is equally possible that the very mixed nature of cottage gardens, where there might only be one or two of each kind of plant, baffled pests which honed in unerringly on the massed displays in larger gardens.

To keep those small gardens endlessly productive, care was lavished on the

Tight planting and crowded quarters don't dismay cottage plants,

which enjoy companionable closeness. What looks like

an artless jumble is actually very well orchestrated,

so that each plant receives precisely the care it requires.

soil. Cottagers often gleaned manure from the roadways, sending the children out with little homemade carts to gather horse and cow pats from public right-of-ways. They also created elaborate composting systems (without calling them that), usually involving materials richer people threw away. Spoiled straw and old fodder, bracken ferns from the woods, garden groomings and similar substances all were stockpiled to enrich their plots. Grit from railway embankments and roadsides was also brought to the garden (often by very young children) where clay soils were common. This opened the heavy soils, improving drainage and air circulation to plant roots.

Cottage gardens make excellent models for modern Americans, because they are much closer in size and scale to our average yard than the vast estate gardens. I still remember the shock of being at Sissinghurst for the first time and realizing that a single border there was longer than the whole city block I lived on. For most of us, the most famous English gardens are wildly unsuitable role models. In contrast, a modest cottage garden combining all manner of plants for year-round needs in a moderate amount of space works far better. Such gardens can readily be adapted to our small yards, whether urban or suburban. What's more, the cottagers' emphasis on organic soil amendments, simple design, and combination of edibles and ornamentals suits many modern gardeners to the ground.

DESIGN ELEMENTS FOR A COTTAGE TEA GARDEN

Sweet with scents and abuzz with busy bees, efficient and hard-working cottage gardens are as useful as they are lovely. Fortunately, they are among the simplest sort of garden to design and make. For obvious reasons, cottage gardens are especially suitable for those who want to create a delightful, beautiful place which has plenty of atmosphere but won't take forever to mature and won't defeat a shoestring budget.

As usual, the primary design principle is that of enclosure. Traditionally, cottage gardens are encircled with stone walls, but if you are short on masonry skills, even a simple picket fence will do. In a cottage garden, enclosure was not so much intended to fence out the world or create privacy as it was meant to make sure stray cows and pigs didn't wander into the beds. Thus, shorter walls and fences were often preferred to tall ones.

Indeed, views into the garden were often deliberately contrived, so that passersby could see just how enormous Grandad's sweet peas were this year. There was an element of showmanship about them, and very often a cheerful rivalry existed between neighbors as each family vied to present the most exuberant floral display to the world. In many ways, these friendly gardens are the exact opposite of the garden retreat; these were garden advances, outgoing places which greeted passersby with a welcoming smile and a flower for their buttonholes.

To achieve this, the enclosing wall was incorporated into the garden, decked with vines and chinked with rock cress and valerian. Any scrap of land that extended beyond the wall was tightly planted for long season bloom, often in a sequence of tough, wiling plants like catmint *(Nepeta)*, Jupiter's beard *(Centranthus)*, pot marigold *(Calendula)*, and wallflowers *(Erysimum)*. This effect is easy to reproduce with low or open picket fencing, where the colorful displays show through the slats from the street.

A well-planned cottage garden produces an astonishing amount

of useful bounty, from tea herbs to fruits and vegetables.

Beautiful soil, well worked and fed with manure, is the secret.

The overflowing effect can be replicated by letting the garden spill through the fencing. Where sidewalk grass strips are available for takeover, the turf (which is often ratty anyway) can be replaced with a gay tapestry of herbs and flowers. In my old Seattle garden, I planted all the parking strips near my house, and when they were full, moved into nearby traffic circles as well. In response, neighbors I hardly knew did the same thing, and soon we were all swapping plants and helping each other weed. This companionable style of gardening has a way of making friends out of strangers, and can unite a disparate neighborhood through the sheer power of plants.

In cottage gardens, the entry is nearly always formalized by an arbor or trelliswork tunnel, which is invariably festooned with flowering vines. Clematis, honeysuckle, roses, and jasmine—both summer and winter blooming—are the usual dooryard plants. In some gardens, a single kind of plant will dominate, sometimes lending the cottage its name. (Places called Jasmine Cottage, Rose Cottage, and so forth are legion.) In others, a rich profusion is preferred, so that entering the garden becomes an intense and memorable olfactory experience.

Within the garden, nonfunctional structure is rare. The strongest lines come from the paths, particularly a wide central path, usually of gravel or beaten earth, which very often bisects the main garden space into two long beds. Generous side paths lead to each house door, and proceed on to the more prosaic back garden, which might hold a tool shed, rabbit cages, and the family outhouse.

Ornamental benches and seats are sometimes introduced, especially as a feature of a grape arbor or rose bower. Traditionally, these were small and extremely simple. Quite often, the only seating was afforded by broad kitchen steps, where the women of the house would sit and shell peas, clean herbs, or peel vegetables. Purely practical work tables and benches were not uncommon, but the English countryfolk were not in the habit of dining out of doors, as their European counterparts often did.

Today, however, al fresco dining—or at least tea-taking—is very much a part of most gardeners' daily lives. Broadening the path into a small seating area and introducing a table and some chairs will in no way make your cottage garden invalid. No garden style which originated in another time, country, and culture can ever be re-created with total authenticity in any case. Cottage gardens, whose abiding spirit is of simplicity, camaraderie, and delight in floral abundance, are highly adaptable. Cottagers were nothing if not resourceful, and many of them would gladly have expanded the scope of their gardens had circumstances permitted.

In cottage gardens, beds were shaped with extreme simplicity. No wandering curves were employed to tease the eye or create visual curiosity in the visitor. If a path curved, it was because it needed to curve in order to reach point B from point A. In such small spaces, it was vital not to waste a scrap of precious earth, and the paths were exactly as wide as practicality (in the shape of cart or wheelbarrow) demanded. Because most allotments were narrow, this meant that the beds, too, were long and narrow. In practical terms, this made them very easy to tend, for no plant was out of reach of the gardener's arm.

A final distinguishing characteristic is less a design element than a practical one, yet it has as powerful an effect on the plantings as any architectural feature could. This is the thorough preparation and ongoing nurturing of the garden

In cottage gardens, seats and benches were placed in sunny spots,

where the women of the house shelled peas or snapped green beans.

As they worked, they enjoyed a cup of herbal tea with their elevenses

(a midmorning snack) or took an afternoon tea break.

soil. In cottage gardens, having all the beds well prepared and planted as full as they could hold was a major point of pride. Few cottagers knew about the value of mulch, so many hours were dedicated to patient weeding. The soil was kept open and fresh through constant cultivating, a practice which involves loosening and stirring the top few inches of soil.

The dazzling displays and densely interlayered beds in these gardens could only succeed if the soil was constantly enriched and kept free of competing weeds. Indeed, the close spacing made it difficult for weeds to squeeze their way in, and daily preening made weeds extremely rare. Cottage gardens were famed for their tidiness, which was the combined result of frequent grooming and natural mulching. The plants' own foliage created a living cover, conserving moisture and suppressing weeds even as they delighted the eye. Marvelously abundant, the cleverly sequenced cottage garden effects made the garden year seem endless. By combining ornamental and edible plants in cottage-style gardens of our own, we too can enjoy an exceptionally long season of flavorful foods, fragrant herbs, and colorful flowers.

PLANT PORTRAITS | *Choosing Plants for a Cottage Tea Garden*

A host of hardy herbs were in constant use in cottage gardens, where they might be called on to play multiple roles, from washing hair and scenting clothing to making up medicines, tonics, and tinctures. Chamomile, for instance, was used cosmetically in shampoo and as a soothing skin lotion, but was also considered a valuable diuretic. Chamomile tea was thought to cure colic, prevent intestinal gas, reduce cramping, and sooth restless invalids.

Healthy people added it to their evening cup of tea to induce a pleasant sleepiness. Rosemary, sage, thyme, and numerous other herbs which today are considered primarily as culinary herbs were similarly used by cottagers to remedy a lengthy list of conditions.

As a result, the small gardens were far more attractive in winter than one might suspect. Mediterranean herbs like rosemary, sage, and lavender will build into large shrubs in short order, especially when given a sunny spot near a path. Rosemary was always placed where it would be brushed by trouser or skirt many times a day and its penetrating, clean scent is an essential part of the cottage garden's distinctive perfume. Sage and lavender were allowed to sprawl unclipped, and their shaggy shapes added structure to the garden when summer flowers were still slumbering.

If left unpruned, these woody herbs can achieve a good size quite quickly, but are apt to get leggy with equal speed. Cottagers kept a steady supply of young plants in the wings by taking cuttings in August and striking them in sandy, gritty soil. When a hard winter carried off the mother plant, one of her daughters was ready to take her place. As a result, these essential herbs were found scattered throughout the garden in various sizes, not placed in orderly, trimmed rows or used as neat edging plants as they might appear in estate gardens.

Indeed, neat edging was never a feature of cottage gardens. Those wide paths were softened by gentle spills of fragrant pinks (*Dianthus*), creeping thymes, and pungent pennyroyal, a carpeting herb which seems almost to appreciate being walked on. Still, since space was at such a premium, rampant herbs like horseradish and spearmint were confined to tubs or old buckets, rather than allowed free rein in the beds.

Although flowers were freely mixed with fruits and vegetables within the long beds, in the front garden and patches that gave onto the road, flowers took center stage. The exact mixture changed from village to village, often including exotic plants from the local "big garden" amongst the humbler blossoms. The roses, however, were apt to be climbers or bushy sweetbriar (*Rosa eglantina*), whose leaves smell so enticingly of cooked apples, rather than stiff hybrid teas.

Long-blooming flowers were favored, especially those which smelled wonderful. Lilies and roses, clematis and honeysuckle, sweet peas and snapdragons are all quintessential cottage garden plants, as are clove pinks, daphne, bee balm, and sweet woodruff. In practice, however, you can vary the mixture according to your own tastes, your budget, and the practicalities of your site and climate. Place each plant according to its preference for sun or shade, moisture or dry soil, and provide plenty of like-minded company. In crowded gardens, overfeeding can create health problems, so it's best to follow the cottagers' lead and feed the soil rather than the plants. Do all this, and the result will provide active pleasure to you and to all who pass your garden by.

BEE BALM

Bees were important creatures for cottagers, whose annual supply of sweetener depended on a happy, productive hive. Bee balm or bergamot (*Monarda didyma*) is beloved of bees, who flock to sip nectar from its clustered, long-lipped flowers. These appear in rounded tufts along the strong, tall stems, which are

Cottage gardens spill their riches out into the road for passersby

to admire (and envy). Gates, arbors, and trelliswork are common entry design features,

always embellished with climbing roses or honeysuckle and clematis.

trimmed with whorls of slightly hairy foliage. Both the leaves and the stems have a potent and intriguing perfume which carries through the garden, attracting our attention even in winter, when only the resting crown is visible. Ordinary soil, full sun, and an occasional drink on hot days are enough to keep this spreading clumper content. Older forms tended to powdery mildew when their roots were dry, but newer varieties like dusky purple 'Prairie Night' are quite drought tolerant once established. Tuck a dried leaf or two into a tin of loose black tea to infuse it with new savor and scent. Fresh or dry, the foliage imparts a sweet, spicy flavor to herbal tea blends.

SWEET CICELY

This cottager's favorite is a pretty, unassuming plant which sows itself about a crowded garden in a modest way, maintaining its presence despite frequent use. Sweet cicely (*Myrrhis odorata*) makes a lacy filigree of foliage in the garden, like a rarefied, ethereal version of tansy, but topped with frothy white flowers. However, if you want to use sweet cicely as a tea herb, keep the blossoms trimmed, or the leaves lose their snap quite quickly. This charming plant grows most cheerfully in partial or dappled shade, and may shrivel or brown off in sunnier spots. Its wants are few and though easily pleased, it is never a pest. The delicate but persistent fragrance is carried in both flower and foliage. Similar to anise but blended with a hint of licorice, sweet cicely foliage has the property shared by artichokes of intensifying sweetness in other foods and drinks. As a tea herb, it can be used as a natural but noncaloric sweetener which never leaves a nasty aftertaste!

A CONTAINER TEA GARDEN

[TEABAGS] ARE A NUISANCE WHEN THEIR

USEFULNESS IS PAST, JUST LIKE PEOPLE.

BUT TO PREFER TEABAGS TO REAL TEA

IS TO EXALT THE SHADOW OVER THE SUBSTANCE.

Anthony Burgess | *The Book of Tea*

Though powdered, instant tea (and even a plain tea bag) horrifies tea purists, an instant tea garden elicits nothing but admiration. The gardenless can change their status in an afternoon, with a single, productive visit to a well-stocked garden center or specialty nursery. Even one large container can provide ground space for a dozen tea herbs. Gather a collection of pots, pack them with compatible plants, and you can start harvesting your first tea crops today.

Container plantings make tea gardens a possibility even in absurdly tiny spaces. Instant tea gardens can be created on any flat surface, from balcony or deck to patio or porch. Indeed, I once made quite a decent herb garden on a steep flight of metal-grating fire stairs reached by climbing out the kitchen window of my minuscule city apartment. (I was a lot younger then, needless to say.) Where no floor room can be spared and only wall space is available, hanging baskets and wall-hung panniers can provide homes for herbs.

When none of these spots present themselves for use, it may be possible to grow an herbal tea garden indoors. Unless large, south-facing windows are available, you will need to provide grow lights to keep your plants contented. Even a small pot garden of flourishing plants is a marvelous treat, indoors or out. It's worth a bit of extra effort to sustain their steady growth, and your care will be rewarded every time you drink a fragrant cup of herbal tea, harvested from your indoor garden.

There are compelling reasons for growing certain tea herbs in pots, even in a large garden. Where winters are wild, many of the invaluable Mediterranean herbs like rosemary and lavender may not survive unprotected. Giving tender

Where garden space is confined to window boxes, teas can be brewed from sage, chives,

scented geraniums, and basils. Here, a wandering spray of hops makes its way into the kitchen window,

offering its leaves and bracts for a drowsy cup of slumber-time tea.

plants a permanent home in oversized containers not only allows us to winter them over under shelter, but can significantly increase the drama of their presentation. A twenty-four-inch-wide pot may stand two or three feet high, elevating everything within it to new heights. Topiary rosemary or standard lemon verbena become sculptural elements when set into large and lovely pots, which may then be moved about the garden as fancy dictates.

Once the last frosts are safely over, tender plants in contained plantings may remain in their garden places from early May until November. To make them as interesting as possible, treat each as a little garden, matching each large tender perennial with smaller foliage herbs, creating leafy compositions that remain attractive for months.

DESIGN ELEMENTS FOR A CONTAINER TEA GARDEN

Healthy plants in good-looking containers can provide a lot of visual pleasure on their own, but we can also work them into the larger garden picture in various ways. Clustered pots by a door or entryway bring a welcoming softness and feeling of life to the hard lines of steps and porches. On decks and patios, pots can be grouped about seats and tables, surrounding us with readily renewable scent and color. Set within beds and borders, containers can become focal points for inner views, or lend structural support to useful but shapeless plantings.

If you aren't sure how to get started with a container garden, begin with some window shopping. Visit several garden centers and nurseries to get a sense of what's out there. These days, most nurseries offer an exciting range of containers, from sleek glazed Thai pots to rosy Italian clay ones. If you don't care for pots, plantable barrels, bins, and boxes abound. You can grow plants in teapots, or even old shoes, if you like.

Traditional places like entryways and porches, stairs and decks, patios and poolsides are far from the only (or even best) placement options. Dramatic, outsized containers are artworks in their own right. Planted with a stunning standard herb, they add instant structure to polite but boring beds and borders. For a quirkier look, tuck small pots between fence pickets or along the top of walls. Line a short path with tiny clay pots, each holding a snippet of thyme or mint. Cluster odd-sized containers on wide sidewalks, or edge a broad driveway with identical and formally spaced glazed Thai pots. Set pots along the edge of a flat roof, or hang baskets from an old clothes line.

Taste is so personal that there are no real rules for creating fabulous container combinations, whether of tea herbs or anything else. However, a few tips may help you to make compositions that please your senses as well as your plants. First of all, find the right container for each plant or combination. Simple pots set off complex plantings beautifully, but highly decorated or intricately shaped pots will look far better hosting a single, clean-lined plant. Many herbs look insignificant without companions, and are most attractive in groups. Big, shrubby ones like rosemary and sage grow best on their own, though they won't mind if you add a shallow-rooted edger like sweet alyssum to soften the lip of the pot.

Herbal combinations are more visually interesting when based on contrasting colors, both of flowers and foliage. To emphasize a certain flower color, add

Contrasts of form help counter the bulky, shapeless quality

of so many worthy but unlovely herbs. Strong verticals from chives or onions

will balance frothy or mounded shapes well.

several contrasting foliage plants. For instance, white flowers look icier against gray and blue leaves, while red ones will sing against burgundy and copper foliage. With herbs, most of the contrast will come from leaves, but some, like calendulas, feverfew, and roses, have significant floral impact, which can be played up with colorful background foliage.

Wardrobe rules apply well to gardens of any kinds. When designing containers, it helps to think in terms of putting together an outfit. Just as with clothing (or even furniture), too much similarity of form can look contrived or boring, suggesting timidity of taste. The most distinctive effects are created when we both match *and* mix. For compositions with greater depth and complexity, mix pastels with warmer shades of the same color: pink with mauve and rose, or lavender with periwinkle and purple. Thyme mats in similar shades can be run together in delightful, tweedy mixtures, while purple sage and blue-flowered hyssop can be mingled with silvery artemisia.

For sparkle, add white to bright color mixtures like clear yellows and blues, using butter or cream for softer blends. Lighten up hot, heavy combinations of smoldering reds, oranges, and purples with silver, gray, and pale blue. It is easy to experiment if you make several pots of similar colors, then play with placement, setting a blue-gray-purple pot near a red-orange-copper one, then adding lemon-gray and another of muted pewtery purple for accent.

As anywhere, variety adds spice to garden compositions. Vivid contrasts of form and texture can do as much as color can to make herb combinations striking. Most herbs offer intriguing textures in or out of bloom, but many are rather shapeless. Use those with stronger form (like spiky rosemary and lavender, spires of lilies, or even chives) to give backbone to plantings with lots of softies. Use an upright plant for a centerpiece, anchored by several mounders and a spiller or two. Lasting attractive combinations offer contrasts of all these factors.

Completing the picture is also important. Oversized containers that hold a standard herb or a shrubby one look more artful when you add a finishing touch. Soften a stern edge with trailing ground covers like golden oregano, or crinkled, dusky bugelweed, *Ajuga* x 'Purple Brocade' (a bugelweed held to be a remedy for liver disorders). A foamy herb like catmint *(Nepeta)*, annual chamomile, or dwarf lavender will also make an elegant edger.

CULTURE TIPS FOR CONTAINERS

To keep your creations looking splendid, a few simple cultural rules will prove helpful. First and foremost is to choose the right soil. Good potting soils are full-bodied yet open-textured. Homemade and inexpensive potting soils are often too heavy, compacting readily with repeated waterings. This makes it hard for air to get to plant roots, which can smother surprisingly quickly in plastic pots. Unglazed clay pots allow more air to reach plant roots; glazed ones can create problems for plant roots if the soil mix is too heavy. Indeed, heavy soils can be fatal in any pots, because there are no worms to aerate them. To lighten heavy potting soils, add generous amounts of vermiculite, a natural mineral that creates air pockets in soils.

Next, choose the right pot. Make sure your container has a hole in the bottom for drainage. If it doesn't, drill a hole or two with a large masonry drill. If you don't want to make a hole in your pot, then consider making it a water jar and growing water lilies. You can also line oversized ornamental pots with two or three inches of gravel, then set your planting in a properly drained pot on the gravel pad. You can hide the gap and disguise the edge of the inner pot with a loose lining of sphagnum moss.

Plastic pots retain moisture nicely and don't break easily. They are rarely lovely, but can always be set inside a prettier one (as above). They are good choices for

Plastic pots offer several advantages over clay,

including lighter weight and greater moisture retention.

Since clay is far prettier to look at, practical plastic pots can be

disguised by tucking them within more ornamental containers.

plants that hate to dry out, like angelica, mints, and speedwells. Clay pots are handsome, but they readily wick moisture out of the soil. Unless they are kept uniformly moist themselves, they rob water from plant roots. Clay pots are a good choice for tea herbs that don't mind being on the dry side, but should still be set into saucers so that you can water them well. Water until the saucer fills, then let the pot sit for an hour or so to absorb as much moisture as it needs. Then you can draw up the excess water with a turkey baster, to avoid root rot problems from too much of a good thing.

As a general rule, avoid peat moss. Peat moss holds water and adds humus to soils, but it also harbors dangerous bacteria which can cause serious health problems. If you handle peat moss, wear gloves and a respirator mask. Another problem is that peat-based potting soils are too light, draining so quickly that the plant doesn't have time to access the water. When peaty soils dry out, they are very difficult to rewet unless you use very hot water, which few plants appreciate. Instead of peat moss, use mushroom compost or aged manure for tilth. A few years ago, you had to make your own potting mixtures to get soil of decent quality, but these days, excellent products abound, thanks to public interest in composting. Indeed, some public utilities are composting garden leftovers, recycling yard wastes into beautiful planting composts.

Once your plants are installed in their pots, regular watering will do more for them than any fancy feeding schedule. Plants in pots dry out more quickly than those in the ground. Many leafy tea herbs won't mind that, but annual herbs in full bloom will. As a rule of thumb, water large containers deeply once a week. Small ones—anything under five gallons—may need water two or three times a week. In hot weather, check all your pots daily. A few inches of mulch helps conserve moisture in pots, as do pot saucers. These catch and hold overflow, giving dry soils a chance to drink deeply. Again, it's best to remove the excess water after the pots have had a chance to take up as much water as they need. Few herbs tolerate standing water.

Herbs planted in good garden soil need little if any feeding, but plants in pots are another story. Most potting soils start out nutritious, but frequent watering leaches the goodness out of the best of them. To keep them growing evenly, put your herbs on a feeding schedule. In spring, a weekly feeding will give growing plants steady support. In summer, a big potful of annuals in full bloom should get fed twice a week.

In addition to frequency, quantity also matters. Most commercial fertilizers are best used at about one-quarter the recommended strength for herbs. This promotes slow, steady growth, which means your combination won't outgrow the pot or lose its proportions. With herbs, excess fertilizer can also lessen the quality of the essential oils in the foliage, making them less tasty or effective. Since each commercial fertilizer is based on a different formula, use a variety of them in turn to ensure a range of trace elements. To avoid burning plants, never fertilize a dry pot. Water as usual, allowing pots to drain. Remove the excess water with that invaluable turkey baster, then feed each pot.

PLANT PORTRAITS | *Choosing Plants for a Container Tea Garden*

Nearly all tea herbs can be grown well in containers, so long as a few ground rules are observed. Annuals, of course, will need replanting each year, but

In large gardens,

rowdy, running herbs

can be restrained in

decorative containers

to keep them out of

trouble. For more

effective combinations,

add favorite culinary

herbs as well as

long-lasting,

fragrant flowers.

most perennials can be content in a pot for years. Indeed, some will share ground willingly, and can be combined in attractive partnerships. The strongest growers will need periodic division, and all will appreciate an annual overhaul for refreshment of soil.

Finding tea herbs that suit both your palate and your pots is a delightful challenge. An amazing number of herbs offer citrus flavors, from tangerine to kumquat. Lemon is represented by lemon mint, lemon basil, lemongrass, lemon balm, and lemon verbena, all good tea ingredients. Orange, lime, tangerine, and even pineapple flavors can be found in mints, thymes, basils, and many other tea herbs. The rose family provides similarly fruity flavors from rose hips and the leaves of raspberries, strawberries, blackberries, and red currants. Chamomile is in every tea garden, prized for its delicate scent and warm flavor as much as for its soothing properties.

Many tea herbs can grow almost anywhere, but even in large gardens, certain ones earn themselves the constraint of a container planting. All the running herbs (of which there are many) are perhaps best enjoyed in large pots, where they can't smother unwary neighbors or tear through the garden like five-year-olds after a cookie break. Mints leap to mind, because despite their exceptional usefulness, they are dreadful garden neighbors with deplorable manners. Pots restrain their thuggish tendencies, keeping those questing roots where they belong.

MINT (*Mentha* sp.)

Mints come in a multitude of forms and flavors, all of which are staples in most herb gardens. Mother plants can be divided and reset whenever they get too crowded, and the whole neighborhood will benefit from the extras. Spearmint and peppermint are the most common (for excellent reasons), but lemon, orange, cinnamon, and apple mint (which comes in a pretty sage-and-cream variegated form) are delicious tea herbs as well.

LEMON BALM (*Melissa officinalis*)

Another indispensable if rowdy tea herb is lemon balm, whose sweet, mild leaves make a tasty tea base. It sows itself shamelessly, filling the garden with its offspring, which need ruthless weeding out unless you want to start a balm farm. Despite its fecundity, its clean fragrance never fails to lift the gardener's spirits. A gilded form, 'All Gold', is brilliantly yellow in spring, fading to muted gold by midsummer.

SAGES (*Salvia* sp.)

Sages of all sorts improve tea blends, especially the fuzzy gray fruit sage, *Salvia dorisiana*, which smells like fruit salad and tastes like ripe melon, and pineapple sage, *S. elegans*, whose red flowers smell like fresh pineapple. Both are tender in cold climates, and need winter protection or annual replacement.

ANNUAL TEA HERBS

When you are just getting started with container gardening, your whole budget may vanish in a single pot-purchasing spree. If the price of plants dismays you, consider growing annuals the first year. Relatively inexpensive, fast-sprouting, and easy to grow, annuals can fill a lot of pots in a hurry. For the price of a single herb start, you can buy enough seed to grow dozens of plants. This way, you can fill your containers as generously as you like. Sow the seeds in flats, small pots, or directly into their containers. Swap extra seedlings with friends, tuck the seeds into the cracks of a wall or sidewalk, and enjoy a summer of flowers and fragrance.

Since many annuals self-sow, next year's bloom is on the house. Try a few new ones each spring to build up your own seed supply. Annuals only live a single season, so they bloom their hearts out, offering themselves up in an endless cycle of renewal. Their dazzling variety makes it easy for tiny or new gardens to spill over with abundance.

POT MARIGOLD (*Calendula officinalis*)

This cheerful flower often blooms all year (its Latin name means "calender flower"). Use the golden petals in teas to gladden the heart, add them to rice for a golden, saffronlike tint, or sprinkle them over salads, soups, and sauces for rich color and mild bite.

CILANTRO (*Coriandrum sativum*)

The frilly green leaves have a peppery bite that enlivens teas as well as almost any entree or salad. Used in both Asian and South American cuisines. If you have coriander seed on the pantry shelf, try sprouting some; cilantro is what you'll get.

BASIL (*Ocimum* sp.)

There are as many basils as thymes, each with its own variation on the family theme. Try lemon basil (*O. citriodorum*), cinnamon basil (*O. cinnamomum*), sweet basil (*O. basilicum*) or dusky 'Purple Ruffles' basil, which makes a stunning backdrop for orange calendulas. All are tasty tea herbs and can be used in cooking as well.

SORREL (*Rumex acetosa*)

Lemony and deliciously tart, sorrel lends teas a singing citrusy flavor. It can be added to salads or sprinkled on broiled fish. It brings marvelous complexity to garlicky sauces and lightens heavy soups. Sorrel often overwinters and self-sows abundantly.

Densely planted herbs can be lightly harvested all season

without impairing their growth or good looks. For larger crops,

trim the entire plant by a third to a half the length of its stem.

USING THE TEA GARDEN

"DO YOU WANT AN ADVENTURE NOW," PETER SAID CASUALLY

TO JOHN, "OR WOULD YOU LIKE TO HAVE YOUR TEA FIRST?"

WENDY SAID, "TEA FIRST, QUICKLY."

J.M. Barrie | *Peter Pan*

Creating delightful places to grow and enjoy tea herbs can feel like a terrific adventure, for each creative design idea has a hidden power to carry us far past our original modest intentions. How many lives have been forever altered by a garden? Too many to count, and all of them fuller, richer, and overflowing with equally countless rewards. The quest for the perfect tea blend is similarly exciting, for each day, the garden's bounty suggests some variation on a familiar theme, each season has its specialties and perfections, and each year, new plants become available to experiment with.

We can enjoy our herbal drinks in hundreds of combinations, changing them at a whim. At first, it's enough just to play about, trying this partnership and that, letting the scent and savor of each leaf direct our choices. Over time, we develop preferences and favorites which we want to repeat and preserve. Keeping a small garden notebook will greatly assist your researches, however casual they may be. You need not take voluminous notes or record every detail of each blend, but nothing is more frustrating than creating a new flavor that everybody adores, then finding yourself unable to replicate the recipe. Simple notes, written as you gather and blend, will prompt your memory reliably when you want to repeat your success. Don't forget to record your reactions to each attempt, even the duds, for your own responses are the best possible guide in the garden as in the kitchen.

How and when we gather our tea harvest depends on where we live. When I gardened back East, I harvested many herbs in late spring and early to mid-summer. Here in the cooler Northwest, we may begin using our herbs in spring, but harvest time often doesn't arrive until July or August for the shrubby

Mediterraneans, which revel in heat and light. In general, the goal is to pick foliage herbs (dill, basil, oregano, and so forth) just before they bloom, when the leaves are mature and full of essential oils. Floral herbs, like chamomile, calendulas, and rose petals, are picked when the flowers are fully open and ripe but have not yet begun to shatter or fade. Hips and haws and seeds are gathered in late summer or autumn, when they are fully ripe and not yet beginning to shrivel or turn moldy.

To harvest your bounty, choose a still, warm morning, after the dew has dried. Take your shears and head for the garden, seeking herb plants at their peak of ripeness. Most of the tea herbs, including marjoram and mint, savory and sage, basil and oregano, tarragon and rosemary, can be clipped over lightly once or twice a month all summer. Frequent but minor trims are productive enough to keep most households well stocked, and will stimulate fresh crops of leaves for next time. Heavy attacks can leave plants too damaged to respond, causing loss through slow disease or sudden death.

To begin, shear each plant loosely, reshaping the shaggy bits and shortening any lank stems by half. On shrubs, this summer shearing promotes healthy, bushy second growth which has time to ripen before fall frosts arrive. On annuals, it promotes multiple flushes of flowers and new foliage to fill the daily teapot well into autumn. Annual and tender perennial herbs are treated in much the same way as perennials and shrubs, except that the final harvest can strip the plants completely. Leaves that are too old and tough for tea can be used for extracts and oils or in potpourri and craft projects.

As I work, I keep a bucket of fresh water and a stack of old tea towels at my side to hold the cut stems and foliage. As I finish working with each kind of herb, I dip the harvested bits in the water to rinse off any dirt, then spread the pieces evenly in the sun to dry for winter use. Stemmy ones like rosemary and thyme can be picked as whole branches and bunched, as can leafier basil, dill, and so forth. If you are new to herb gathering, it will prove helpful to write the name of each herb on a file card and keep it with the towel. Once the leaves are dry, they all look pretty much the same, and some even smell quite

Sages of many kinds, from the pink and purple clary to wide-leaved

culinary types, perform excellently in pots. Over time, perennial or shrubby kinds will require

larger homes, but young plants enjoy good company in a well-filled pot.

similar. Labeling immediately helps keep your supplies in good order all the way down the processing line.

To store your harvest, let the leaves dry well, either in the sun, or in a slow oven, or even the microwave. This last approach may only take seconds, so proceed with caution until you find the right settings. Once dry, I prefer to store tea herbs in bottles, where they won't get dusty or be munched by mice. You can also double-bag and freeze herbs for up to six months with no loss of flavor. Flowers can be dried on racks or in the oven or microwave as well.

Since thicker pieces sometimes dry unevenly, I use small sachets of powdered milk in each jar to absorb any extra moisture, which would cause the flowers to mold. (You can also use the small desiccant packets that come with vitamins.) The same technique works beautifully with dried seeds. Pretty as they are, those herb jars don't belong on a sunny windowsill. Store them in a dark cupboard, as exposure to light can break down their stored oils.

Seeds can be harvested as soon as they are evenly ripe but before they tumble to the ground. Certain plants (such as chervil and borage) cast their seeds around the garden with enthusiasm, while others (like angelica and holy thistle) are beloved of birds. To be sure of a good harvest, you can bag ripening seedheads with little sacks made of muslin or cheesecloth. Paper bags rot in rain, while plastic ones can promote mildews and molds, so cloth is definitely the material of choice. If you are not a seamstress, you can seal the bag edges with duct tape or even staple them loosely around each seedhead. When the seed ripens, it falls into the bag, which is airy enough to keep it from rotting or sprouting too soon. When you want to harvest, you just cut away the bags and remove the seed. Some seeds need cleaning before use or storage. If a lot of chaff comes with the seeds, you can dry them on paper plates, labeled with the herb name. When the seeds are dry, you can softly sift them with your fingers, blowing gently to waft away the chaff. The clean seeds can be packaged in coin envelopes (labeled immediately so you don't forget) or in jars. As with flowers, include dry milk powder sachets to prevent mildew.

Tea herbs can also be harvested on a daily basis, with no thought for tomorrow. My favorite time to make fresh herb tea is early in the morning, after the kids are off to school, but before the day's work has begun. I take my teapot into the garden, filling it with snippets of whatever catches my eye. I fill it with simmering water, let it steep a bit, then find a spot to sit with it, out of earshot of the telephone.

Brewing teas directly in the pot can cause a golden brown patina of tannin to build up inside, which passionate brewers believe simply adds to the character of the pot. If this discoloration bothers you, scour it away gently, using a mild abrasive like baking soda, but don't ever use soap in your pot, for it will invariably leave a slight residue that will affect the flavor and quality of your teas. If the delicate stains do not bother you, a hot water rinse will clean your pot just fine.

It is of course possible to brew teas directly in a cup, using a strainer of some sort. Tea balls, which hold dry tea leaves, can also be used in a teapot to keep the tea leaves from clogging the spout. However, most strainers and tea balls are too small to allow for proper expansion of dried herbs, which will double or triple in bulk when moistened. Unless they have enough room to swell up, their full flavor won't develop.

In my experience, the tastiest tea results from pot-blended herbs steeped in plenty of hot water. Here's my best advice: place fresh or dried herbs in an ample teapot. If you have time to warm the pot first, add hot water, drain it, then add the herbs, cover them, and let them absorb the steam for a minute before adding water again.

Next, bring water to a simmer—not a rolling boil, which robs the water of oxygen, leaving it flat and devoid of sparkle. Pour the simmering water into the pot, measuring at first, until you know how full your pot will be when you add two or four cups or water (or whatever quantity you habitually use). Let the mixture steep as long as need be; this will vary from one or two minutes for blends which contain Japanese green teas and fresh herbs to five or six minutes for dried herbs with hips and seeds. Use a strainer when pouring out each individual cup.

Iced or chilled teas are best made from cold water, which renders a clean, unclouded mixture that shimmers in the glass. Use slightly more dried or fresh herbs for cold teas, and steep them in glass containers to prevent off flavors from developing. When you serve cold teas, you may find it easier to sweeten them with simple syrup (made by boiling sugar and water) than with granular sugar, which doesn't dissolve well in cold liquids (neither does honey). If your tea is too strong, you can dilute it to taste, adding cold water or seltzer to make a flavored spritzer. Cold teas can be garnished with a sliver of lime and a sprig of mint; and ice cubes made with your tea blend, limeade, or any minty tea base will add a cooling clink to the glass without weakening the flavor.

Drinking homemade

tea in the midst

of a sunny garden

provides a simple but

extremely satisfying

pleasure. What you put

in your daily pot

will vary with

mood and season,

yet always bear

the hallmark of

your own taste.

HERBAL TEA RECIPES

TEA IS PROPER BOTH FOR WINTER AND SUMMER,

PRESERVING IN PERFECT HEALTH UNTIL EXTREME OLD AGE,

AND IT MAKETH THE BODY ACTIVE AND LUSTY.

Thomas Garraway | *England's first purveyor of tea (mid-seventeenth century)*

In my garden, our daily teas alter with the seasons, depending on the herb garden's current best bets as well as our own inclinations. Weather, too, has an influence—a breezy, sparkling blue morning might call for a cheerful blend of orange mint, raspberry leaves, and lemon balm, while damp, gray afternoons demand a more stimulating brew of anise hyssop (which tastes like mint and red licorice), bolstered with sprigs of spicy bee balm and a bite of sweet-hot cinnamon basil.

Lashing downpours call for sterner measures, such as a brisk and incredibly aromatic cup blended from rosemary, lavender, and lemon verbena, a bright, sassy brew that will leave you singing in the rain. The first snow earns a celebratory cup made from mashed rose hips, lemon thyme, and a single leaf of horehound. Evening tensions ease away under the influence of steeped catnip, red clover, St. John's wort, and pineapple sage.

Serious herbalists may combine several dozen herbs in a single blend, carefully balancing emphatic flavors with mellow ones, brightening a deep-toned mixture with brisk citrus and mellow mint, or adding body and depth to light blends with a touch of culinary herbs or bitters (thus that single leaf of horehound). However, utterly satisfying teas can be made from simple combinations such as red currant leaves with chamomile flowers, or lemon balm and spearmint. Indeed, some people prefer herbal teas with just one ingredient. It's wonderful fun to play with enticing combinations, but in the end, your own taste and pleasure should dictate what you put in your teapot.

Before introducing this chapter's recipes, I feel inclined to add an often-cited quotation, taken from *The Art of Simpling,* a manual written by William Coles in 1656. He says of his work, "I have in it communicated such Notions as I have gathered, either from the reading of Severall Authors, or by conferring some-times with Scholars, and sometimes with Country people; to which I have added some observations of mine Owne, never before published: Most of which I am confident are true, and if there be any that are not so, yet they are pleasant."

Here, then, are my herbal tea offerings, including both dried blends and snip-as-you-go combinations straight from the garden. In each case, serving quan-tities are indicated by the number of cups of water to be added to the herbs. If you want to make a single cup, or less than the amount indicated, blend all the herbs as listed, either in a zip-closure bag or in an oversized bottle to allow for proper mixing. You can then measure out enough for as many servings as you desire (a single cup nearly always requires a heaping teaspoonful). Small, single-serving teapots brew one or two cups better than a tea ball or strainer (which rarely allow for full expansion of the dried herbs) but either method may of course be used. You can also make the full amount and save the extra to serve iced, or invite a few friends to take a convivial cup with you.

A quiet tea break brings calm into the busiest life.

Even the smallest gardens have room for a snug corner

for contemplative or restful tea-taking.

HUMMINGBIRD TEA

Red as rubies in the cup, this pretty blend looks like hummingbird syrup.
It also features flowers which attract hummers in the garden; red-flowered
pineapple sage (Salvia elegans) *and blue anise hyssop* (Agastache foeniculum).

2 tsp fresh *or* 1 tsp dried rose hips, lightly mashed

2 tsp fresh *or* 1 tsp dried pineapple sage flowers and foliage

1 tsp fresh *or* ½ tsp dried anise hyssop flowers and foliage

Cover the herbs with 4 cups of simmering water. Let steep for 3 to 5 minutes. Serve warm or cold.

PICK-ME-UP TEA

Savory and bright, with a snappy, mildly peppery bite, this brisk afternoon tea
has a broth-like quality that makes it especially comforting on a cool spring evening
or a foggy autumn afternoon.

2 tsp fresh *or* 1 tsp dried fruit sage (*Salvia dorisiana*)

2 tsp fresh *or* 1 tsp dried chamomile

1 tsp fresh *or* ½ tsp dried lemon thyme

1 tsp fresh *or* ½ tsp dried cilantro

1 tsp fresh *or* ½ tsp dried parsley

1 tsp fresh *or* ½ tsp dried calendula petals

1 tsp fresh *or* ½ tsp dried sorrel

1 leaf fresh *or* dried horehound

Cover the herbs with 8 cups simmering water. Let steep 3 to 5 minutes. Serve warm.

ENERGY PLUS TEA

*We modern folks need a lot of extra energy just to get through our busy days.
Taking time out for tea will help restore flagging energy levels, especially if
the tea is this one. You can grate the fresh ginger root or just put young buds
through a garlic press (you don't even need to peel them).*

1 tsp fresh *or* ½ tsp dried ginger root

1 tsp fresh *or* ½ tsp dried marjoram

1 tsp fresh *or* ½ tsp dried sweet woodruff

1 tsp fresh *or* ½ tsp dried goldenrod

1 tsp fresh *or* ½ tsp dried basil

Cover the ingredients with 5 cups of simmering water. Let steep for 3 to 5 minutes. Serve warm.

SWEET DREAMS TEA

*When daily tensions mount and sleep seems far away, a quiet cup
of warm tea can calm jangled nerves. These traditional sleep inducers will
ease the transition from wakefulness into relaxed, deep sleep.*

1 tsp fresh *or* ½ tsp dried catnip

1 tsp fresh *or* ½ tsp dried chamomile

1 tsp fresh *or* ½ tsp dried lemon balm

1 tsp fresh *or* ½ tsp dried hops

1 tsp fresh *or* ½ tsp dried lemon thyme

Cover the herbs with 4 cups of simmering water. Let steep for 3 to 5 minutes. Serve warm.

MOCK EARL GREY TEA

True Earl Grey tea is a blend of fruity Darjeeling black tea with oil of bergamot, a Chinese bitter orange. A traditional substitute is herbal bee balm (Monarda didyma), which has a similarly spicy-orange flavor and aroma.

2 tsp fresh *or* 1 tsp dried Darjeeling tea

2 tsp fresh *or* 1 tsp dried bee balm

Cover the ingredients with 4 cups of simmering water. Let steep for 3 to 5 minutes. Serve warm or cold.

TUMMY TAMER

Upset tummies can bother adults as well as children. Sufferers of any age will draw comfort from this pleasant concoction, which has an especially enticing fragrance.

1 tsp fresh *or* ½ tsp dried fennel

1 tsp fresh *or* ½ tsp dried bee balm (*Monarda*)

1 tsp fresh *or* ½ tsp dried burnet

1 tsp fresh *or* ½ tsp dried sage

1 tsp fresh *or* ½ tsp dried anise seed

1 tsp fresh *or* ½ tsp dried spearmint

1 tsp fresh *or* ½ tsp dried peppermint

1 tsp fresh *or* ½ tsp dried basil

Cover the herbs with 5 cups of simmering water. Let steep for 3 to 5 minutes. Serve warm.

THROAT SOOTHER

Native Americans used wintergreen (Gaultheria procumbens) *to soothe rough, unhappy throats before the Europeans arrived. It was quickly adopted by the colonists, who appreciated the pleasantly minty flavor of the foliage in an age when most medicinals tasted extremely nasty. This tea tastes good enough to tempt children, who will probably want some honey added for extra sweetness.*

2 tsp fresh *or* 1 tsp dried wintergreen

2 tsp fresh *or* 1 tsp dried fruit sage *(Salvia dorisiana)*

1 tsp fresh *or* ½ tsp dried lemon thyme

1 tsp fresh *or* ½ tsp dried sweet cecily

1 leaf fresh *or* dried horehound

Cover the herbs with 6 cups of simmering water. Let steep for 3 to 5 minutes. Serve warm.

TRIPLE MINT TEA

For mint lovers, this combination is as good as dessert. On a hot day, try it iced, with limeade ice cubes. Some people prefer the snappier bite of peppermint to the smooth, mellow spearmint, so here, too, it's good to play around with several combinations to find your favorites.

2 tsp fresh *or* 1 tsp dried chocolate mint

2 tsp fresh *or* 1 tsp dried orange mint

2 tsp fresh *or* 1 tsp dried spearmint

Cover the herbs with 6 cups of simmering water. Let steep for 3 to 5 minutes. Serve warm or iced.

GOLDEN FUTURES TEA

*Gilded foliage makes this tea especially pretty when fresh leaves are used.
Fresh or dry, the combination is soothing to stressed nerves, making the
present look rosy and the future bright with promise.*

2 tsp fresh *or* 1 tsp dried golden sage (*Salvia officinalis* 'Aurea')

2 tsp fresh *or* 1 tsp dried golden feverfew (*Tanacetum parthenium* 'Aurea')

1 tsp fresh *or* ½ tsp dried golden oregano (*Origanum* x 'Aureum')

Cover the herbs with 6 cups of simmering water. Let steep for 3 to 5 minutes. Serve warm or cold.

⤞━◆━○━◈━⤝

ROSE HIP, FENNEL & ARTICHOKE TISANE

*The tart bite of rose hips is balanced by the brisk, warm savor of fennel
and the natural sweetness of artichoke pulp. Rugosa rose hips are especially
fat and tasty (and loaded with vitamin C), though almost any kind will do.
For the artichoke extract, save the tough, outer leaves from your dinner artichoke,
scoring them lightly or slicing them in strips before making the infusion.*

¼ cup fresh *or* 2–3 Tbsp dried *Rosa rugosa* hips

2 sprigs fresh fennel leaves *or* 1 tsp dried fennel foliage

4 artichoke bud leaves

*Assemble all ingredients in a teapot, cover with 4 cups simmering water. Steep for 3 to 5
minutes, serve plain or with herbal honey for extra sweetness.*

SUMMER SPARKLER

*This sweet, sunny blend is excellent hot or cold, and smells extraordinarily good
either way. Gunpowder tea comes in little balls which expand with a great release
of savor and scent. Since green teas steep very quickly, experiment to see
how strong you like it: a mere minute might be enough.*

2 tsp fresh *or* 1 tsp dried gunpowder or pan-fired green tea

2 tsp fresh *or* 1 tsp dried rose petals

2 tsp fresh *or* 1 tsp dried orange mint

*Cover the herbs with 4 cups of simmering water. Let steep for 1 to 2 minutes.
Serve warm as is, or cold with a dash of tonic water over ice.*

>+>+O+<+<

JASMINE-SCENTED TEA

*On a snowy or rainy day, this smoky, sweetly scented tea blend will warm you to your toes.
The delicious perfume smells especially exotic in cold weather, though warmer temperatures
will reveal more of its subtleties.*

$1/4$ pound pan-fired green tea

2–3 Tbsp dried *Jasmine officinalis* blossoms

1–2 tsp grated dried lemongrass

*Blend all ingredients, sifting well to mix. Store in a tightly sealed glass jar for up to 2 months.
To store it longer without losing freshness, pack the loose tea in several thicknesses of freezer
bag, replace it in the jar, then refrigerate or freeze the container. To use, infuse 1 teaspoon tea
blend in 1 cup simmering water for 2 to 3 minutes. Strain and serve at once.*